metaphoria

POEMS & MEDITATIONS

GARY WOOD

Bainbridge Island Press

POEMS

meta

MEDITATIONS

phoria

GARY WOOD

Bainbridge Island Press

Bainbridge Island, WA

Metophoria: Poems & Meditations
By Gary Wood
Copyright © 2023

Published in 2023 by Bainbridge Island Press
Bainbridge Island, WA
https://bainbridgeisland.press

Printed in the United States of America

ISBN: 978-1-961451-04-9
Library of Congress Control Number: 2023950204

Designed by Ben Rockwood

9 8 7 6 5 4 3 2

Dedication

My gratitudes, like beatitudes, are several:

First, to my offspring: Jason, Jarret, Juliana & Joy, each of whom have inspired me, challenged me it differing ways through my journey of parenthood and whose beautiful cluster of noisy offspring that keep pointing me toward a hopeful future and thus give me further reason to live.

To an extending family that includes differing families of origin, differing personhoods and differing understandings of life, but who come together frequently and so remind me that we are WE, and that is a treasure.

To Donna, a sister who reads my words and is sometimes touched with tears of appreciation; To Frank & Tim, my most loyal and supportive man-friends who truly know me, soulfully, and encourage me in the flood of words and questions that flow through my heart and mind.

Above all and especially, to Sandy, my favorite artist, partner, and forever love... who lets me please her and still keeps her feet upon the ground, letting me fly safely in her surrounds.

....And most recently to Tamarah and Ben, new friends who see me and venture the hard work of publishing this, my first book.

Contents

metaphoria

POEMS & MEDITATIONS

GARY WOOD

Prologue

Kindergarten: Learn the Code

Pressing down too hard
another pencil-point snapped-off,
another crumbling gouge
into the soft kindergarten paper,
staying between two lines...

Sweating with effort,
forearms sticking to his desk, the page

To copy the letters...
again, again, one by one...

Learn the code... Learn the code!...

Birthing himself
  with great labor
    into the world of words...

Little did he know, how could he know...
so long, long ago...
the doors becoming opened
to meanings, to wonders,
to existence, would ever so unfold?

Poems

This Poetry

This poetry
'tis a blessed-madness
demanding her ample due,
a voice from the innermost-outermost...
incomprehensible
gloriously beyond the simple mind's eye to see...

This poetry,
words cast into the void
words retrieved, gilded,
bloodied from heartfelt living...
words telling the many stories
words telling the one great story-yet-told.

This poetry,
lifting the heart from darkness and dread,
the hand moves, the soul stirs,
life returns, as if from the dead...
the reborn knowing
that we know things
so far beyond the words...

This poetry,
a grapple with the wildness
making torrid with the muse
who will not lie down for long...
like the passion of procreation
you did not beget
you will not conclude...

This poetry,
a craziness of the unleashed heart,
running around, over, through
the bounds of mind

Lost In the Wonder

Becoming lost in the wonder,
outrageous wilderness,
passionate life all around,

We travel our own particular journey
and venture into the heights
and the depths
of being alive....

So celebrate this birthing,
this beating heart...
celebrate Life that just wants to keep on...

We are souls
clustered, traversing in similar arcs
through a universe-being-created
at and for this time!

Wildman

Like a wildman,
he relishes the sun upon his skin
feels the vigor in his veins
amongst the trees
the stream-current's song in his ears.

Like a wildman,
fir cones, needles, twigs and stones
under a naked foot
the faint smell of pitch
perking the nostrils
the elements, his element.

Like a wildman,
his rising, the sun's rising
the wobbling earth,
her seasons revolve
his moods, his desires also revolve
playing to her cycle's dance.

Like a wildman,
inhaling smoke
the tribal-circle fire
river-rinsed hair now dry
char-smudged hands
tearing open giftings offered
by the family, oh greatest gratitude
for all laughter shared tonight;

Like a wildman,
without words, he listens, placid-smiling
gazes into the embers,
watches sparks clamor skyward…
the midnight clear
star-studded infinity
expanding overhead
he prays in silence
to what he can never understand

Write!

As if nothing else matters more than the moment,
jotted down perchance someone's future reading
shall evidence that you were here...

Write!

As if the message of your existence be unfolding,
obscure, pure, true, should come out, incomplete
but suggesting the sacred haunting, as a ghost...

Write!

As if no one shall ever know you, the creature embodied,
breathing, watching, listening, who's heart found some purpose
beating out that which cannot be understood...

Write!

Cathartic Pen

The cathartic pen
bleeds black upon the white
convulsive fits and starts
breaks forth, halting, bitter
damning all cohesion...

Without apology, the hand coughs up
words of destitution unrestrained
raking savage the field,
oh, rotten stalks of inspiration
strewn with sharp stones and tangled brambles
oh, taunted man who cannot lay down and rest this night

Ink-well

He can write, he must write
to wrap his fingers loosely, tight
around the pen, he contends to hold
as the ink-well of his soul
and so the words come forth, messy, bold

And as his hand becomes consigned in servitude,
be placed upon the barren page, itself becomes imbued
with fitful scribbled words, as well as it can
as if to encrypt some languished sounds…

Musing up from someplace else, someplace old
the words murmuring, abound from all around

And he finds himself become a-mused, as well, surprised
as the words themselves come forth as if alive
with an insistence to be heard beyond the noise, as if alone
and the writing goes not where he controls…
seeming to have a will, a soul, of its own.

Surrendered

And the pen, in turn grasps him by the hand
and casts him down upon the bed of wonders
and takes him over as if an urgent lover
a shower of whisperings under cover

And as he surrenders unto her essence charm
the words flow like a fitful thunder storm
raindrops, pelting upon the panes outside
sorrows, recognitions, regrets abide
Things known now, not before
his history seen: an open door
'seems now but just a fool let loose upon the world

He writes anyway and spills his ink out
upon the white of this universe, a craziness of being
not bound in this enhardened concreted-world...
And as he allows, she overtakes him still, draws down
into his breath, into his core and fills his heart again...

Hollow Reed

The pen be but a hollow reed, he holds
as if mythic ink be flowing from reservoirs unnamed, untold
as it writes itself out these words, be they sputtering, be they bold

A squiggled group of lines in ink, upon a page
as if a presence, voicing an inner sage
shows itself as fleeting, urgent, yet ruthless, unafraid

For even as we daily dwell in myriad minds
our daily hungers within, reside
we expend our time, so busy about our tasks and blunders
we are yet blessed to stumble into worlds of wonder
and follow the trails of ink, perhaps our pathway home

The Explanations

The explanations line up
further than the eye can see,
one behind another…
all true, all false,
begetting the next in line…

We tarry our consciousness
upon the present one
and move on, in due speed
toward no end.

First Man I Loved

Call her cruel, call her kind
great Nature has her way with him, today
with fitful slumber, awakened glances
gestures to the one true lover who remains,
partners, both still graceful to the end.

Now others come and go
to check the vital signs, attend the dose and flows…
some friends, family circulate
with soft and courageous words.

First man I loved, did indeed adore,
the recalled memories of the forgotten years
I lived as a lucky son

Then Was Gone

He died just last evening's fall
breathed his last, and then was gone...

We gathered small in the corner of his room
his body lay... he was not there...
and talked some of how to honor his passing

This morning broke...anyway
a sun rose bright and clear
and the earth turned on
with all of its noisy life

I thought... as indeed, it should.

Opened Window

At the quivering border of ecstasy
we hang as from slender threads
staccato breaths hover as over
roiling furnaces within…
and by a mere fleeting glimmer's light
I peer through your open window,
you through mine…

Separation's illusion be interpenetrated!
while our bodies dance
to the great writhing rhythms
as they are so made and prone,
…(by something akin to god)…to do!

Nose Dive

Seeing the trajectory…
propulsion, majority expended now
arc-turned-into a nose-dive
some time ago

White-knuckles, weightless
gripping, jerking a broken stick…
pilot, navigator, passenger, one…

My illusions!… my illusions..!
Did I really think that I could fly?

September

Ah, September,
your mellowing season
stream-flows waning
brush hinting of the scarlet show
just to come...

Winding down,
days shortened
each sunset sooner than before
the rays seem somehow warmer
amidst the cooler airs

A pondering place
the summer's surge of life
concluding...
with quieting pause
the tick of time just spent
and settle in.

Half Blind

On occasion, when to ponder with feeble mind
either interstellar or subatomic endless space,
to see this wafer-slice of in-between,
wherein lies all distinctions…time, illusions shared
…our meeting place:

Marvel this en-raveled mystery,
interconnected knots of reality… where together,
we hold this space in which each freedom's will can act
to make some things matter and some things not,
choosing to be separate, alone, while always reaching out
toward the all-forgotten fact:

That all threads in the fabric of what we can know,
both warp and weave, crisscrossing patterns
of Universal mind are spun from the one same fiber,
from out of the nothingness as creation pulses on,
spinning its thin veil, in which we live, half-blind.

Native Roots

Ah, the skin reminds me of my Nature's native roots…
naked on a rock among the cedars, blue sky,
the river's churn, sun glistening
through a squinted, sweat-wetted brow

Forget me not, my Mother, and I not you…
born of this sand, this rock, smelling the season's glories
We listened to your rhythms…our clans sheltered along the
banks of rivers such as this.

How many men before have gazed across the waters
and heard a current's song?

How many have bathed in the Father's sun
and felt the swirling breezes 'round the ribs,
the thighs, the mind?

Wrinkles

Running the iron over the blouses and pants,
she presses flat the wrinkles and tells me everyday tales
of her wrinkled senior friends who gather and share
the tragic circus-comedy of their aging...

Inspired by their joviality, their care shared,
the courage lifted by those who, with effort, still stand,
teetering, and who choose each other's company,
shedding all pretense of who they are
and laugh instead of cry.

I begin

I begin to see the emerging light
and see it is invisible to the eye, the mind
unseeable to any distracted, busied mortal soul..

Its vastness so overwhelms my processing
as infinity abounds in all directions

Awe.... Awe.... is everywhere!

'Tis the eventual ultimate reverence.

Still Dawning Minds

For eons before
we grunted and groaned
first sounds of our dawning primate-minds
the budding tongue, the budding brain
generations of curiosity pulling ourselves along
we sing a stirring song, without refrain
evolution's restless quest of Becoming,
birthing distinctions, the naming of things
the thinking of thoughts, of what is and is not seen
and what is all the rest, in-between

The wonderment is our cause, beyond explanation
we play in our own garden of Creation
reason is our tool, not the answer
Awe is the purpose of our still-dawning-minds

Words Begetting Words

Words begetting other words,
expanding minds, ceaseless questions over time
we keep speaking them, are never enough
defining themselves by each other,
their answers always as if standing,
precarious, on some horizon's bluff

The more we know,
the more we know we do not know
a single soul reaches out forever
into the mystery, beyond all history
remembering ourselves incompletely
still probing, guessing into our deepest dreams
we create the path as we travel upon it
as it is, or as it seems

The words follow along behind our wonderments
futile expressions, metaphors conquer all explanations
definitions proliferate, the dictionary of existence
grows and grows without end, as we
enjoin this dance with Infinity

Ordinal Source

The creative force, our ordinal source
cannot be fully channeled
the whole truth, yet disentangled
cannot get through

We are always living
on partial faith, partial fact
nothing be known for sure
and we are yet together, life must interact

Still moving on, moving through
our journeys through time, our lives to do
yet somehow find some ways to share,
to create a single world of me …and you.

Let it be

So, let it be in your inner revelations
as if someone, something else were speaking
showering you with thoughts and words
stirring up Nature's senses in your private world

The sounds of winds whistling in the trees,
the surf crashing upon its shores
a twittering eagle soars
a raven calling cawing, winging free

Reminding you of greater worlds, imagination's opened doors
yea, spoken with greater words than these...

Dribblings

So, let your upwelling intuitions, notions
come out incomplete, as dribbling thoughts and words
without need of defended cause or explanation...

Let them show themselves stumbling, mumbling
in their clear or cloudy self-reflection
it matters not if they even suffer misdirection

Let them put their feet upon their ground
to see if they find some gravity in your heart, your mind
that some truth is pushed forth to be begot
with no sense that these truths are true
and must be milked for all their worth,
no sense that they should not...

Mere Words?

'Sometimes strange, sometimes awakening
how mere words assemble their unique successions
collections of flowing thoughts and recollections
some splurging constellations of loose associations
that take us into new spaces, new places
never known before…

And what 'mere words' are these??

Like a Plow

Like a plow, the pen be as haltering
through a field of stumps and stones
chunks snagging upon the roots and bones
of silent things, near-forgotten, things of yesterday's life
A plow moves some days deeply in crooked ways
turning up things becoming deadened, yet not rotted away

Like a plow, the pen reveals what is beneath
the ground we tread, and turns over our percolated soils within
at last to breathe, to speak and face a generous sun again
and so too the clouds, and the rains come, as well
and release a delicious ancient bionic spell
telling stories and words that call things back to Life again!

So fertile yet still be the enduring earthen-sphere,
where poems become witness, as if stewards of the cycles here,
so dear to breathe in the pungent airs, the fragrance of our possibility,
our cause of hope, undeterred, of Life and living
vital worlds …and vital words.

Pleadings

Some aspiring metaphors
plead us to look somewhere higher
and lift us, in our words and worlds of passion's fire
show us, inspire us of what could be
beyond the realm of our certain gravity

We speak in sounds and symbols of that spark within
and Creation throbs in the heart of paradox and possibility!

Words Thrown

Sometimes we throw our most sacred yearning-words
toward that something that can't be written, be said, be heard
as if inspiration's voice become silenced, frozen, dead instead
as if some murmured fleeting notion be too holy, too true, to grasp

And so, if wise, we bend the mind, wait patiently, trust the future,
trust the past and vacate the noise, be still inside, be with the place
we are at last, beyond our thoughts, breathe long and slow and know
that we do not know

And permit the near-frozen liquid strictures to melt and flow within
be suppled, changed in the heart, as seeds to grow
the laws and rules become wizened, alive with love,
transformed, to awaken softly the sleeping hand, again
as well, the ink, the words, the pen

Limitations

We think our Consciousness.
is a mere human discovery,
our invention
a marvel to ourselves...

Not pre-existent,
not infinite,
not creative, expanding,
not inclusive of it All...

And we are limited by our thinking

The Creative Urge

The creative urge keeps raising its bloodied head…
there is no defeat, no end to the primordial Idea from which we
sprang

Yet our breaths of curiosity and wonder be certainly numbered
each day's creative acts and thoughts some day shall end,
a foreshortening by one of the numbers remaining,
themselves, our individual fates uncertain…

So, we have our own time-limited opportunities to celebrate!

…Or not…!

Only Poetry

It can only be said in poetry,
often only spoken in synergistic metaphor
the mind still forever be casting off its primordial mud
grappling with its 'literal' world and words…
always thinking thoughts, as one thinks one should
making and solving problems that spur further problems

We are still but rudimentarily wired, determined to know,
to understand, to interpret the meanings of everything
explaining, explaining away the magic …
'So tragic..!

Yet the heart knows without understanding
is always beating, its trusted rhythms
always seeking, the joys of reaching,
exploring the marvels of imagination,
looking out into the great wonders, traveling far
only to find and return to our connection, together
finding home…

All Spokes

All spokes be of the same wheel that forever turns,
the circle, spiraling around about again
ever deeper into the mystery

We circulate on an infinite perimeter
repeating itself, always new,
around a mobius axis we can never see
but know is there

We look out, we look in…

We sometimes find ourselves
grasping for the same essential thing
the discovering that we are but including
and excluding, without concluding

Restless

We cannot rest
from the tales and the telling
of the endless stories
of ourselves, of those before

We speak in different tongues
since those ancient many yesterdays
before we became apart
but yet still belonging together,
toward the ancient remembering…

That… Our origins are only One…

Bloom

We are but buds of consciousness
seeded, newly arisen from the darkness
so unaware of our immaturities,
we do not see through our own obscurities
and notice just a glimmering hint
of the expanse of Infinity

So much room and need, there is to bloom!

Denial

Past the denial there is the roiling anger
striking out, revulsed by the possible picture
of our own, self-made, demise

Past the seeking, the demanding of miracles
the hopes and prayers, expectations to be manifested
as if some gift to us, by science, technology, if not by god itself

Past the arguing, the bargaining, the shaming, the blame
for our distracting addictions, all measures of self-inflictions
to escape the hosts and ghosts of deflected pain...

Life has its hardships, no one is protected, favored, no one excluded
from their part of creating the circumstances of our existence

All, we are participants in a life in which we try to deny our presence,
our effect, our own cause that we stir within Creation's endless stew

'Tis it, our choice to concoct a self-made elixir of paradise?
......or stir up an apocalyptic brew?

How Profound?

How profound, how banal
these words stand up with all passion's initial might
but lay down amongst the crumbling earth
under stumbling feet, afraid to come out into the light

I am…I am not: awake, asleep
and the clock ticks, the heart beats
another moment's past
just like the last

Who cares?.. Who cares, even I?
that I forever am always asking 'why'?

Ho-hum!.. I am yet be done!
This nonsense madness bores me still…
deeper yet it seems my hum-drum random muse
uses, yea abuses whatever comes her way

Slave to her indulgence, her disguises
she toys with me, disappoints, surprises

She commands the hand to move
and speaks her nonsense
as long as I will listen

My ears ringing, senses tingling, numbing
I slump toward my slumber
more wasted time, wasted ink!

Inspiration

Inspiration flows
from a something greater as I open to it…

I am in the midst of an ongoing creation,
magic still underway... The everyday miracle
keeps evolving, the Now is all the time, everyday

Everything is changing,
the world is always in a grand wholistic play
How could I possibly complain,
be bored in any way???

Destined

We are destined to hurt one another
clumsy in our seeking,
needy in our fears…
The human creature, full of foibles,
sometimes full of tears

Apologies and forgiveness's
are our salvation, antidotes to our loneliness,
animosity and ruthless wars
we are challenged in this brief living
before we return unto the stars

Beyond Understanding

It is always beyond understanding
and so there be tortures and confusions

And so there be marvels and joys…

Reasons and explanations are over-rated.

The Veil

Open to the essential recognition
that we have union, we have the collective "I"…
looking out, over, across…
finding eyes looking back
at oneself
through the Veil.

The Nightmare

The nightmare
is that your offspring
shall have never really known you...

That your foibles, flaws
and egregious blunders
will turn them away
before they come to shoulder their own life
learn to forgive your parentage
and see into your heart

Dancers

We are dancers, apart,
swirling in the eddies of each other's lives
feeling the currents, the fluids roiling…
as we gaze into the auric wonders
of each other's souls…

Field of Play

This
is the field of play

This
is where we find ourselves
meeting up,
carrying through
the agenda of our souls.

Flux

Move off your arbitrary center
only an inch or two…

Free-fall, but only for an instant,
and your reference shifts…

Fixity finds fluidity in her natural form…

All things be changing,

Flux be the rule.

Superstitions

We anthropomorphize the magic
as it freely flows,
and bring it down into our fearful minds

And bury ourselves
in superstitions and endless rules.

This Living

All souls become
wounded by this living…
No one escapes the piercing…

Yet we breathe on,
pick ourselves up from the shards of our doings
and find we are still here

And that is what we choose…

Free Dog

Free dog roaming the wood
sniffing out the burrows and the droppings
that drift amongst the brush

The winter blows cold,
the air is crisp
the wondrous whiffs of things unseen all about

Unleashed, alone in the thicket
another cycle turns…
ragged, some scars, trusting yet
for another season to follow his nose

I am, instead
fumbling with my thoughts and words
wondering who is the gifted one?

Fulfilled

No man can stop the feeding frenzy,
except his own…

Those voracious ones who step
straight into the middle of the bounty
and take until the pains of competition
or consumption bring them down

There will never be enough to go around
if we cannot declare, in truth,
"enough" for ourselves
and step back, in peace, fulfilled.

Downstream

Downstream…
All things travel downstream

What we cast into the currents
are washed away, downstream.

Some other time, some other place
debris, find your resting space, downstream

The river carries someone's yesterdays
another's tomorrows...

I stop to sip from the waters,
and pause, …downstream

Innocent Poetry

Watching little girls,
scamper across the rocks...
the rushing waters swirl all around
hushing with deafening sounds
except squeals of delight,
as they turn, start or meet
on the rocks,
balancing
like innocent poetry
in bare feet
stringy hair
in the back-lighted sky
over a mountain,
the girls and I

No Idea

He has no idea
what I'm talking about
deaf to the music, the mystery
of inspiration's lofty notes and scores
something beyond his world,
of dry logical thoughts and conclusive words

The dream too big,
the chasm too great, ...too great
I stammer and ramble,
my words, my thoughts constrained
on the stage of a tamped-dry
non-imaginal world
of brick-by-brick reality,
roads and walls,
our simple fate

I should save my words
for more open ears...

Or I should rain...
and rain... and rain...
without relent
and just see
where life may grow...?

The Allure

Darkness long fallen, he warms a final cup, anyway...
climbs into the nest with books, pad and pen to follow his
wonderings this night.

Underlined phrases, entrusting some wisdom to the author
who speaks to him tonight... the knowing of soul
transmitted through words, encouraging him to step out
into his own world and create a life
rooted in the true and honest ground within

Never-mind ennobled understandings gathered thus far,
which dance, clumsy-footed in the background...

Never-mind who would judge his erroneous foolishness
unworthy of what this time...

Never-mind the crumbling facade of some conformity
thrown off into the underbrush, naked in the wilderness,
his self-made fire issues warmth beyond the chill of
scrutiny's eyes

The universe unfolding, growing, changing
Infinity teasing onward....

Ah, the awareness of this one fool, so stupid
of vast facts, meanings, understandings, yet glimpsing the Whole,
beyond his mind, no words depicting
that which is only seen obtusely, fleetingly...

Crackling embers, ideas sublime, the attempted reaching
capturing grasp into the airs
always opens empty-handed...

Ah, the Allure... the Allure...
in bed, looking upward, outward, inward,
homeward, with Allure

The Soup

Playing in the mix,
the Grand soup of all thoughts
and ideas preceding,
we build hope upon vanquished fears,
trials and tears, the biting spices,
the renderings of love, the sweetness of fruitful affections
and earthen roots and spices, all stirred in.

Flavors be changing over time,
ingredients added, servings drawn off to fuel the journey,
always stirring, always brewing
being careful of what's included today,
to be consumed tomorrow and tomorrow

Paradox

The words make you soar
and bring you down
firmly into the earth…

Paradox,
in one line of poetry
turns the heart,
turns the mind
inside out

Meditations

Without wonder
there is only
the known and the unknown..

Nothing
that calls out to the other side

———◆———

Everything is created

Nothing is left out.

The idea, "perfection",
is only an idea, non-existent…
the illusive possibility
always dancing beyond reach

We advance and recede, never arriving…
the counter-flow necessary
such that the field of polarities
be held open
permitting us a space between
to live and aspire to something better

———◆———

Inspiration
means aspiration
means perspiration

Without difficulty,
nothing would be out of reach.

The work before
prepares for the work to follow…
There is no other track
than the track I am on

One step follows another…
all the way, every day
I only know what is before me
and who I have come to be over this time

If I say 'no,' I can only eventually say 'yes'
the choice is to move forward and discover,
move forward and discover, move forward and discover
…or delay…

———•———

One who speaks
reveals more ignorance
in themselves, than wisdom…

So let us talk much and long,
my friend
and be humble

Forget the words
for they are but symbols and sounds

Remember they are only conjured
struggling to represent
the notions, their histories, experiences:

Otherwise, un-sayable…

———•◦———

Do not be afraid, my friend
to speak, to pen your mightiest thoughts
to let your spirit soar to unknown heights.

Do not be afraid to let your heart sing, take flight
to voice the song in which you thrive

Do not be afraid to be Alive!

What fool
doth come upon his own shadow
sometime past midnight...
and not invite him in,
draw him close to the hearth
to chase the chill away?

———◆———

We choose what we choose
We get what we get

We attach value to certain things
more than others...

We choose what we choose
We get what we get

We juxtapose things
and force them to mean
what we need them to mean…

And the mind,
for a very brief, peaceful time,
is pleased

———◆———

To those who push ahead into the line

I say to you, your competitiveness and tenacity
has served well in the survival of our species…

And now, serves well our own demise

Regrets
follow you
like a hungry dog...
close at heel,
under your elbow,
wet, smelling foul,
crawling into bed with you at night

———•———

"It's just
your imagination!"
they will tell you,

...cutting
at the jugular of your power

Bearing no scars, no wounds
it has healed itself,
in an instant's beating

Of a forgiving heart...

———•———

There are those moments when you feel
"<u>THIS</u> is what I am living for!"

And there are those other many moments...

One who is yet
to be humbled by life
steals the fruits of the Garden
and remains, still
without any wisdom of the soul

———•———

It is always beyond understanding…
And so there be tortures and confusion
And so there be marvels and joys

Dropping the pretense of knowing,
Confessing to be an utter fool...
Then, for an instant, we Know...

———•———

We frolic with gravity
And sometimes, we fall down

The Great Paradox
Is and isn't true

———•———

Nothing is as simple as it seems

The extremes are necessary
for there to be freedom
In between

Knowing not what to do,
We do nothing…

Doing nothing seldom informs us any further

———◆———

Afraid to act
We come to a standstill in the middle of the freeway,
Assuring certain catastrophe

We want to strike a bargain
And give over only a part of ourselves to Life...
And so we are cheated by our own withholding...

———◆———

Oh ridiculousity!
Are you strutting out for all to see?
Or crouched, on the couch, being smaller than you are?

Possibility expands the self...
Do not deny her.

All things be likened to all things…
Parts inclusive, the whole always expanding
Beyond the reaches of mind

We are conscious to only some small degree
As to who we are
And what is happening here

———•———

The unthankful heart grows smaller
and yet again smaller

All are blessed, all are wounded...
And so what shall we make of our own circumstance?

———◆———

Be not puzzled by the puzzle...
Wonder will suffice

More than anything else,
We should know that we know not much about any-
thing…
But mostly, we do not even know that

———•———

Possibility speaks…
And what is your reply??

Accept the darkness, the horror of now
Include, expand…
And contemplate Possibility

———•———

Nothing of the past
Prevents the possible-future

The past sets up for the future but does not determine it..
Cause happens right now...

———◆———

Futility
Holds the hand at bay,
Stops thought, mid-sentence,
Cares not for anything...
Shrivels the soul.

Without wonder,
There is only the known and the unknown…
Nothing that calls out to the other side.

———•———

Waiting is a waste of time…
Sometimes, it is the best you can do.

What fool proclaims
That he is not also one?

———◆———

What genius be not confused by infinity?

What if we were to turn all this talk
Of our success and acquisitions
Toward the joy of this just Being here?

———•———

This is the destiny to which we have come...
Yet nothing of the future can be contained...

There is always Possibility...

We are burned up in the process of life
The color of the flame is in how we fuel it…

————•————

Simple things become complex…
Then simple again.

Each breath permits the evolution to succeed,
The future to unfold
The Origin to be fulfilled…

———◆———

The way of the heart
Does not make sense to the way of the Mind

We do what we do...
'oft-times with reason clamoring along behind

Trying to make sense of it all.

———•———

The practical situation
Wakes up to meet you,
Every morning...

All of our moments
Have led to this moment…
And we are here, Now…

———•———

Always we tread the path
Of our own work…

There is beauty!...
We recognize it when we see it.
And it becomes prevalent throughout the universe
As we look for it...

———•———

If it is the time of awakening...
How could we not yearn to be a part of it?

The messages come through to us
As we are willing to listen…

———•———

It's the appetite… Not the food…

If the universe is shrinking,
fear and loss are our most natural companions…

If expanding,
all transitions move into higher form,
all waves roll into greater seas…

———

Consciousness creates
the something from the nothing,
makes patterns in the chaos,
forms order, assumes will and stirs desire
breathes life into our heart
and heart into our life.

One who does not celebrate

Suffers...

———◆———

There is nothing apart unto itself

Nothing not included

Coda

Still Here

And so, yet we are still here
kicking at the clods of dirt and broken stones
beneath our toughened calloused feet
our journey has taken us down many roads
sometimes together, sometimes alone
sometimes bitter, sometimes sweet

And the sun is rising up this morning,
the breath of Life is still passing through our nostrils
a new day opens before us now

About the Author

Gary Wood achieved an advanced degree in clinical and developmental psychology and came to Washington State in 1975 as a counselor and mental health programs manager. He was especially drawn to interests that were nested in the nature and origins of human consciousness and navigating the vast spectrum of individual differences in talents, personalities, beliefs and how we come to understand ourselves... and each other.

Over time, this curiosity grew beyond career-focused contexts and led him into vast personal explorations of relevant sciences, classic & contemporary philosophies, theologies, and stories of a few notable authors, theorists and characters of history. As well, he periodically engaged a few trusted guides, therapists and skilled facilitators to reveal his own willful and/or unconscious perceptions and false notions within his own still evolving psyche.

He took notes along the way, more as reference points and reflections than any sense of intended future authorship. But, over time, his questioning seemed to morph into insightful dialogue and some strange sense of wisdom and truthfulness emerged. The writings began to reflect some authentic need to give poetic voice where words say things that cannot be said otherwise.